DiSGUSTiNG JOKES

Gigglers

DISGUSTING JOKES

Toby Reynolds

Illustrated by
Andrew Pinder

■SCHOLASTIC

Scholastic Children's Books
Euston House, 24 Eversholt Street
London NW1 1DB

A division of Scholastic Ltd
London ~ New York ~ Toronto ~ Sydney ~ Auckland
Mexico City ~ New Delhi ~ Hong Kong

First published in the UK by Scholastic Ltd, 2015

Text by Toby Reynolds
Illustrations by Andrew Pinder

© Scholastic Children's Books, 2015

ISBN 978 1407 15246 2

Printed and bound by CPI Group (UK) Ltd, Croydon, CR0 4YY

2 4 6 8 10 9 7 5 3 1

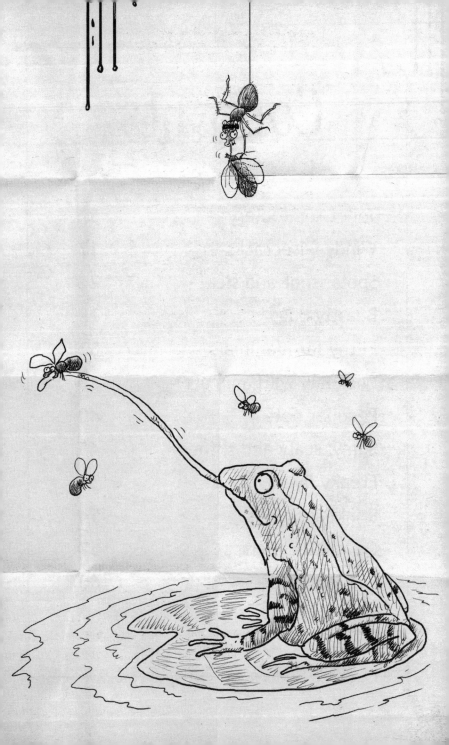

Contents

Toilet tomfoolery

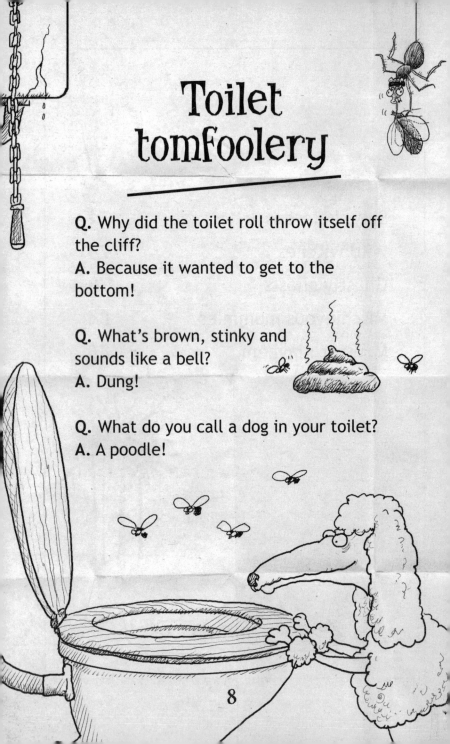

Q. Why did the toilet roll throw itself off the cliff?
A. Because it wanted to get to the bottom!

Q. What's brown, stinky and sounds like a bell?
A. Dung!

Q. What do you call a dog in your toilet?
A. A poodle!

Q. What vegetable grows in a toilet?
A. A leek!

Q. When does 'q' come before 'p'?
A. At the public toilet!

Q. What did one toilet say to another?
A. You look a little flushed!

Q. Why do English teachers spend so long in the toilet?
A. They are always writing poo-ems!

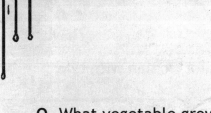

Q. What do you call a woman with two toilets on her head?
A. Lulu!

Q. Did you hear the joke about the toilet?
A. Never mind, it's too dirty!

Q. What day of the week do most people get diarrhoea?
A. Splatter-day!

Q. Why did the beach smell bad?
A. Because the sea weed!

Q. What's the best way to keep flies out of your kitchen?
A. Keep a bucket of manure in the hallway!

Q. Have you heard about the new book *Constipation*?
A. It hasn't come out yet!

Q. Why did the nerd take toilet paper to the celebration?
A. Because he was a party pooper!

Q. Why did the child tell the toilet a joke?
A. Because she thought it looked down in the dumps!

Knock, knock.
Who's there?
Europe.
Europe who?
No you are!

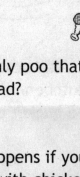

Q. What's the only poo that doesn't smell bad?
A. Shampoo!

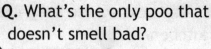

Q. What happens if you brush your teeth with chicken poo?
A. You get fowl breath!

Q. What's brown and sticky?
A. A stick!

Q. What do you call perfume made from diarrhoea?
A. Eau de Colon!

Q. What type of tree can't you climb?
A. A lavatory!

Q. What did William Shakespeare think when he sat on the toilet?
A. To pee or not to pee… that is the question!

Q. Why was the footballer banned from using the bathroom?
A. He was always dribbling on the seat!

Q. Which swashbuckling heroes liked to urinate on their enemies?
A. The wee-musketeers!

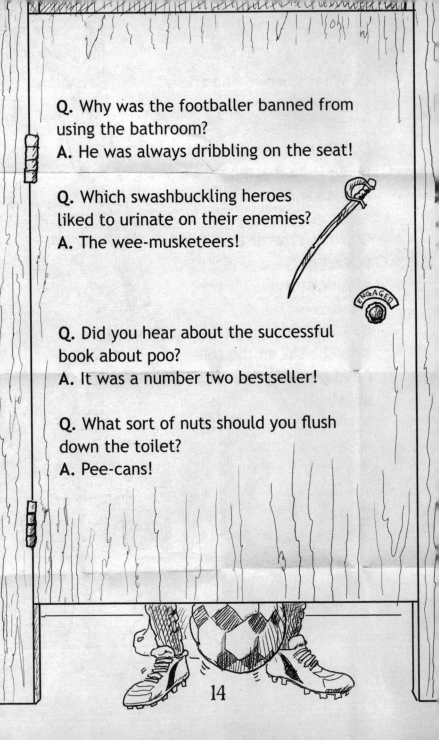

Q. Did you hear about the successful book about poo?
A. It was a number two bestseller!

Q. What sort of nuts should you flush down the toilet?
A. Pee-cans!

Q. What happened to the plumber who found a million pounds in the sewer?
A. He got stinking rich!

Q. Did you hear the gossip about the giant with diarrhoea?
A. It's all over town!

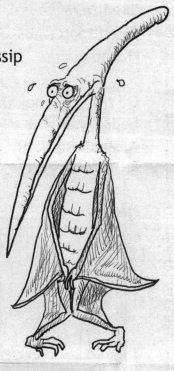

Q. Why can't you hear a pterodactyl going to the toilet?
A. Because the 'p' is silent!

Q. What's the difference between roast beef and pea soup?
A. Anyone can roast beef...

Q. Did you hear about the constipated maths teacher?
A. He worked it out with a pencil!

Knock, knock.
Who's there?
Smell mop.
Smell mop who?
Hahahahaha.

Q. Why did the madman hide under the bed?
A. Because he thought he was a little potty!

Windy wisecracks

Q. What is the sharpest thing in the world?
A. A fart. It goes through your pants and doesn't even leave a hole!

Q. What is it called when the Royal family farts?
A. Noble gas!

Q. What does the Queen do after she burps?
A. Issues a royal pardon!

BURRRPP!

Pardon me

Q. Which king used to break wind at the dinner table?
A. Richard the Lionfart!

Q. Which queen always burped at the dinner table?
A. Queen Hic-toria!

Q. What has a bottom at the top?
A. Your legs!

Q. What do you call a very windy dinosaur?
A. A Stinkosaurus!

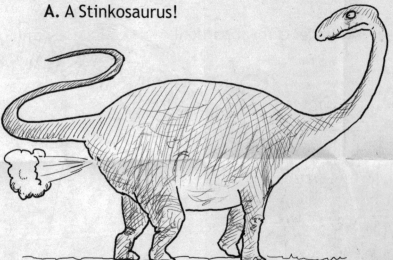

Q. Why did the astronaut suffocate?
A. He farted in his spacesuit!

Q. What is the cheapest way to take a bubble bath?
A. Eat beans for dinner!

Q. Who smells the worst at weddings?
A. The farter of the bride!

Q. Which fairy is the smelliest?
A. Stinkerbell

Patient: Doctor, I have dreadful wind, can you give me something for it?
Doctor: Yes, you can borrow my kite!

Q. What do you get if you cross a birthday cake with a can of beans?
A. A cake that blows out its own candles!

Q. Why is your nose in the middle of your face?
A. Because it is the scentre!

Q. Who is the smelliest royal in the world?
A. King Pong!

Q. What do you call it when someone breaks wind in a time machine?
A. A blast from the past!

Knock, knock.
Who's there?
Gas.
Gas who?
Gas who just farted!

Q. What is invisible and smells like bananas?
A. Monkey farts!

Spots, snot and sick

Q. What's the difference between bogeys and broccoli?
A. Kids won't eat broccoli!

Q. How do spots get into shape?
A. They do zit-ups!

Q. What did the nose say to the hanky?
A. Well, blow me!

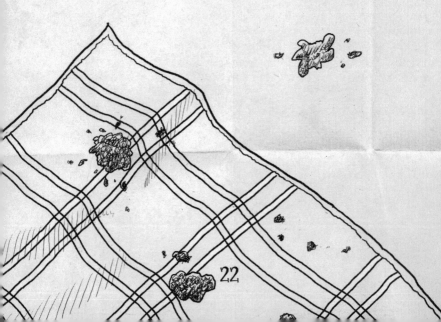

Q. What did the clown say after sneezing?
A. Snot funny!

Q. Where do Spanish people go to vomit?
A. Barf-celona!

Q. How do you make a handkerchief dance?
A. Put a little bogey in it!

Q. How did Captain Hook die?
A. He picked his nose with the wrong hand!

Q. What's more disgusting than eating your own snot?
A. Eating someone else's snot!

Q. Why is it hard to keep a criminal with acne in jail?
A. Because he's always breaking out!

Q. How do you know if a boy was made upside down?
A. Check to see if his nose runs and his feet smell!

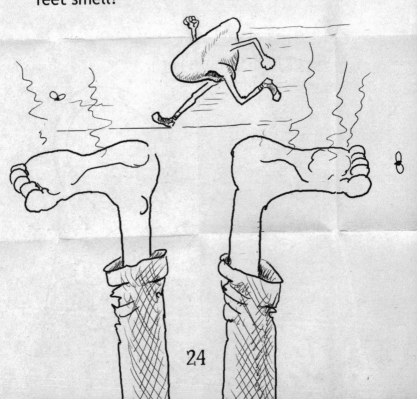

Q. Who is the boss of the hankies?
A. The handker-chief!

Q. Why do old people always put their hands to their mouths when they sneeze?
A. To catch their teeth!

Q. What is green and hangs from trees?
A. Monkey snot!

Q. What's black and white and red all over?
A. An exploding zebra!

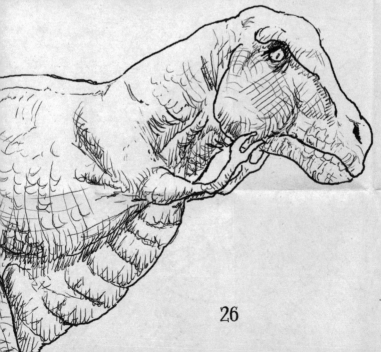

Q. What do you call a row of bogey-eating boys?
A. A picket line!

Q. Which dinosaur kept being sick?
A. Tyrannosaurus Retch!

Q. What is the difference between Brussels sprouts and bogeys?
A. Children won't eat Brussels sprouts!

Q. What monster gets stuck to the end of your index finger?
A. The bogeyman!

Knock, knock.
Who's there?
Police.
Police who?
Police wipe your nose, it's all runny!

Beastly bugs

Q. Why is the letter 't' so important to a stick insect?
A. Without it, he'd be a sick insect!

Q. How do you find out where a flea has bitten you?
A. Start from scratch!

Q. What airline do fleas prefer to travel on?
A. British hairways!

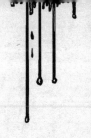

Q. What happens when fleas become angry?
A. They get hopping mad!

Q. What do you call a cheerful flea?
A. A hoptimist!

Q. What do you call nits on a bald man?
A. Homeless!

Q. What did one flea say to another?
A. Shall we walk home, or wait to catch a dog?

Are we there yet?

Q. What did one nit say to the other?
A. I'm going to go on ahead!

Q. How do you turn ants into underwear?
A. Put a 'p' in front of them!

Q. Why was the little ant so confused?
A. Because all his uncles were ants!

Q. What did the strawberry say to the maggot?
A. You're boring me!

Q. What's worse than finding a maggot in an apple?
A. Finding half a maggot!

Q. What did the maggot say to the apple?
A. It's been nice gnawing you!

Q. What is the definition of a caterpillar?
A. A worm in a fur coat!

Q. Why was the glow-worm unhappy?
A. Because her children weren't that bright!

Q. What do you call an evil flying insect?
A. A baddy long legs!

Q. Why did the fly fly?
A. Because the spider spied 'er!

Q. What do you call a fly with no wings?
A. A walk!

Knock Knock.
Who's there?
Amos.
Amos who?
A mosquito bit me!

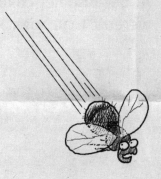

Filthy farm animals

Q. What has eight legs, four eyes and flies?
A. Two cows in an aeroplane!

Q. What would you get if cows could fly?
A. A pat on the head!

Q. What do you call a boy who stepped in a cowpat?
A. Dung-can!

Q. What do you give a pig with a rash?
A. Oink-ment!

Q. Why do you call a pig that is a master of karate?
A. A pork chopper!

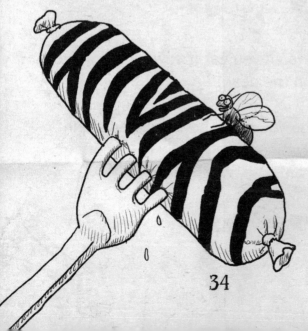

Q. Why didn't the pig let her piglets play with toads?
A. She didn't want them to become warthogs!

Q. What do you get if you cross a pig with a zebra?
A. Stripy sausages!

Q. What do you call a haunted chicken?
A. A poultry-geist!

Q. What do you get if you cross a hen with a dog?
A. A pooched egg!

Q. What happened to the farmer who tried to cross a lion with a goat?
A. He had to get a new goat!

Q. Why is it so hard to have a conversation with a goat?
A. Because they keep butting in!

Wickedly wild animals

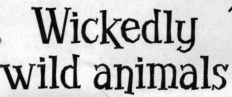

Q. What do you give an elephant that feels sick?
A. An awful lot of room!

Q. How does a lion greet other animals?
A. So pleased to eat you!

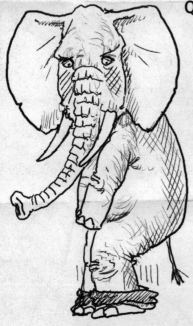

Q. Why were the elephants arrested when they went swimming?
A. They couldn't keep their trunks up!

Q. Which day of the week do lions attack people?
A. Chewsday!

Q. What do you call a bear with no teeth?
A. A gummy bear!

Q. What do you call bears with no ears?
A. B

Q. What do you call a reindeer that burps in your face?
A. Rude-olph!

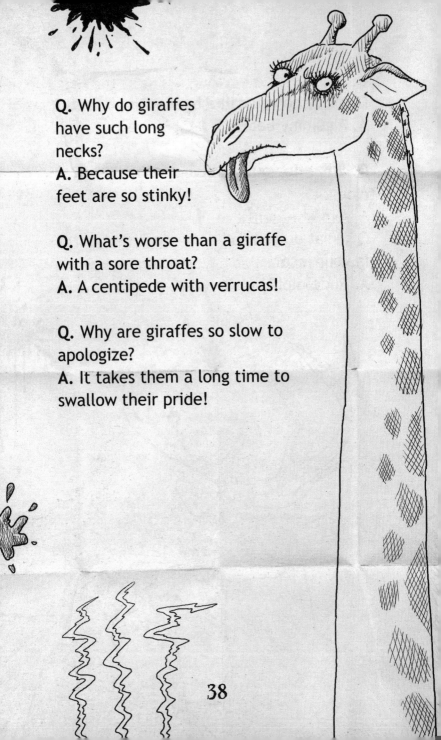

Q. Why do giraffes have such long necks?
A. Because their feet are so stinky!

Q. What's worse than a giraffe with a sore throat?
A. A centipede with verrucas!

Q. Why are giraffes so slow to apologize?
A. It takes them a long time to swallow their pride!

Q. Who stuck their tongue out at the Big Bad Wolf?
A. Little Rude Riding Hood!

Q. What has antlers and sucks your blood?
A. A moose-quito!

Q. Why do gorillas have huge nostrils?
A. Because they have large fingers!

Peculiar pets

Q. What did the dog say to the flea?
A. Stop bugging me!

Q. Why did the dog poo cross the road?
A. It was stuck to the chicken's foot!

Q. What do you get if you cross a soldier with a dog?
A. A Pooper-trouper!

Q. Which type of dogs have the most ticks?
A. Watch dogs!

Q. What did the dog say when he sat on the sandpaper?
A. Ruff!

Q. Where would you find a dog with no legs?
A. Wherever you left him!

Q. What happened to the dog who ate nothing but garlic all day?
A. His bark was worse than his bite!

Q. What breed of dog always has a cold?
A. Achoo-wawa!

Sniff

Q. How do you teach a dog to fetch?
A. Tie a cat to a stick!

Q. What do you have to avoid when it is raining cats and dogs?
A. Stepping in a poodle!

Q. What do cats call hummingbirds?
A. Fast food!

Q. What happened when the dog visited the flea circus?
A. He stole the show!

Q. What do cats like to eat for breakfast?
A. Mice Krispies!

Q. What happened to the cat that ate a ball of wool?
A. She had a litter of mittens!

Q. Why did the cat put the letter 'm' into the freezer?
A. She wanted to turn ice into mice!

Q. How do you make mice smell nice?
A. Use mousewash!

Q. What's soft and white on the outside and grey and furry on the inside?
A. A mouse sandwich!

Q. What did Mrs Mouse say to Mr Mouse when he broke his teeth?
A. Hard cheese!

Knock, Knock.
Who's there?
Rabbit.
Rabbit who?
Rabbit up carefully,
it's a gift!

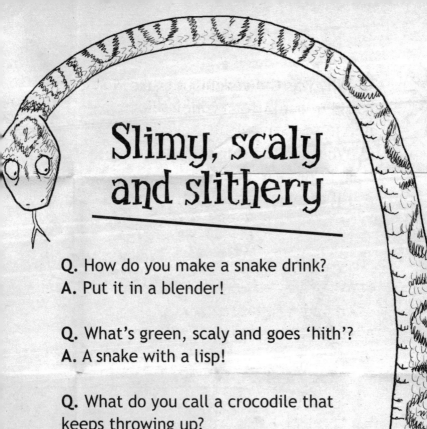

Slimy, scaly and slithery

Q. How do you make a snake drink?
A. Put it in a blender!

Q. What's green, scaly and goes 'hith'?
A. A snake with a lisp!

Q. What do you call a crocodile that keeps throwing up?
A. An ill-igator!

45

Q. Why was the venomous snake worried?
A. He'd just bitten his lip!

Q. What did the slug say after the other slug hit him on the head?
A. I'll get you next slime!

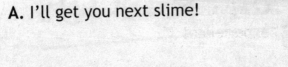

Q. What does a toad say to a friend he hasn't seen in a while?
A. Warts new?

Q. How can you revive a dying snake?
A. With mouse-to-mouth resuscitation!

Q. What is a frog's favourite drink?
A. Croaka Cola!

Q. What happens if you kiss an electric eel?
A. You have a really shocking experience!

Q. What's green and covered in red spots?
A. A frog with measles!

Q. Why are frogs so happy?
A. They just eat whatever bugs them!

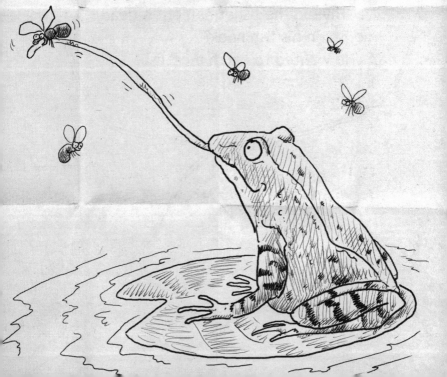

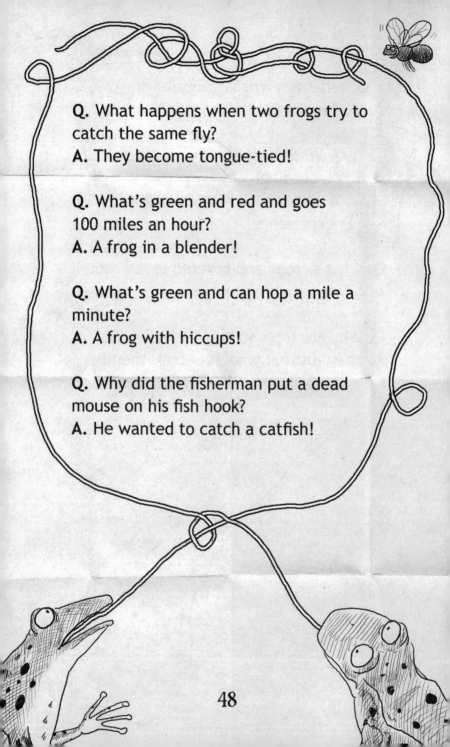

Q. What happens when two frogs try to catch the same fly?
A. They become tongue-tied!

Q. What's green and red and goes 100 miles an hour?
A. A frog in a blender!

Q. What's green and can hop a mile a minute?
A. A frog with hiccups!

Q. Why did the fisherman put a dead mouse on his fish hook?
A. He wanted to catch a catfish!

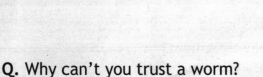

Q. Why can't you trust a worm?
A. They always wriggle out of everything!

Q. What type of fish can't swim?
A. Dead ones!

Q. What do you call a fish with no eyes?
A. A fsh!

Q. What is the definition of a slug?
A. A homeless snail!

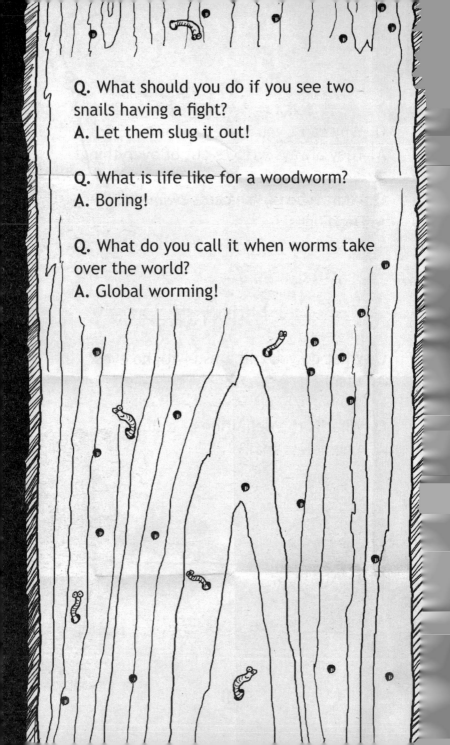

Q. What should you do if you see two snails having a fight?
A. Let them slug it out!

Q. What is life like for a woodworm?
A. Boring!

Q. What do you call it when worms take over the world?
A. Global worming!

Freaky flyers

Q. What flies around your light at night and may bite your head off?
A. A tiger moth!

Q. What did the gardener get when he ran over a bird with a lawnmower?
A. Shredded tweet!

Q. What did one vulture say to the other?
A. I've got a bone to pick with you!

Q. What do you call a woodpecker without a beak?
A. A head-banger!

Q. Which villains steal soap from the bath?
A. Robber ducks!

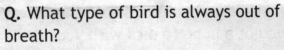

Q. What do you give a canary with diarrhoea?
A. Tweetment!

Q. What type of bird is always out of breath?
A. A puffin!

Q. What do you get if you cross a snake and a bird?
A. A swallow!

Q. What's the worst thing that could happen to a bat while it's sleeping?
A. Diarrhoea!

Knock knock.
Who's there?
Who.
Who who?
Is there an owl in here?

Stinking skunks

Q. Why did the skunk take an aspirin?
A. Because he had a stinking cold!

Q. What do you get if you cross a skunk with a boomerang?
A. A terrible stink that keeps coming back!

Q. What do you call a flying skunk?
A. A smell-icopter!

Q. What happened when a skunk robbed a bank?
A. The police were soon on his scent!

Q. What's a skunk's favourite game?
A. Ping-pong!

Q. How do you stop a skunk from smelling?
A. Hold his nose!

Q. What do you get if you cross a mole with a skunk?
A. Smelly tunnels!

Q. Why are skunks so clever?
A. They have a lot of scents!

Q. What do you get if you cross a skunk and an elephant?
A. I'm not sure, but you can smell it coming for miles!

Q. How many skunks does it take to stink up a room?
A. A phew!

Q. What do you get if you cross an owl with a skunk?
A. An animal that stinks, but doesn't give a hoot!

Knock Knock.
Who's there?
Butternut.
Butternut who?
Butternut stand behind an angry skunk!

56

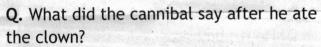

Cannibal capers

Q. What did the cannibal say after he ate the clown?
A. That tasted really funny!

Q. How do you help a hungry cannibal?
A. Lend him a hand!

Q. When do cannibals leave the table?
A. When everyone's eaten!

Q. What happened at the cannibal wedding?
A. They toasted the bride and groom!

Q. What did the cannibal get when he was late for dinner?
A. The cold shoulder!

Q. What is a cannibal's favourite party game?
A. Swallow the leader!

Q. What do cannibals eat on their toast?
A. Baked beings!

Q. What happens when you annoy a cannibal?
A. You end up in hot water!

Q. What do you call a cannibal who ate his mother's sister?
A. An aunt-eater!

Q. What do vegetarian cannibals eat?
A. Swedes!

Knock knock.
Who's there?
Cannibal.
Cannibal who?
Cannibal-eve you're gonna eat me!

Vile vampires

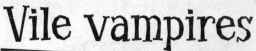

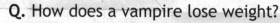

Q. How does a vampire lose weight?
A. By eating necks to nothing!

Q. What is a vampire's favourite flavour of ice cream?
A. Vein-illa!

Q. What do you get when you cross a vampire and a snowman?
A. Frostbite!

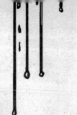

Q. Why is a cemetery a great place to write a story?
A. Because there are so many plots!

Q. What does a vampire fear most?
A. Tooth decay!

Q. Where do vampires store their money?
A. At the blood bank!

Q. Why are cemeteries always noisy?
A. Because of all the coffin!

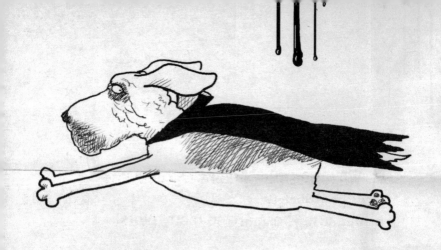

Q. What type of dog does Dracula have?
A. A bloodhound!

Q. What is a vampire's favourite dance?
A. The fangdango

Q. Why was the vampire thrown out of art class?
A. Because he could only draw blood!

Q. Where does Dracula go for a swim?
A. Lake Eerie!

Q. Do vampires enjoy their jobs?
A. Of corpse they do!

Q. What did the vampire say when he left the dentist?
A. Fangs very much!

Q. What is a vampire's favourite fruit?
A. A blood orange!

Q. What is the best way to talk to a vampire?
A. Long distance!

Q. What does Dracula have at 11am every morning?
A. His coffin break!

Q. Where is Dracula's office in America?
A. The Vampire State Building!

Q. What happened when the boy vampire saw the girl vampire?
A. It was love at first bite!

Q. Why can't Dracula play cricket?
A. He lost his bat!

Q. Why are vampire bats like false teeth?
A. They always come out at night!

Q. What do you get when you cross a teacher and a vampire?
A. A blood test!

Q. Why did the vampire get thrown out of the haunted house?
A. Because he was a pain in the neck!

Q. What kind of boats do vampires like?
A. Blood vessels!

Knock, knock.
Who's there?
Ivana.
Ivana who?
Ivana suck your blood.

Q. What is a vampire's favourite desert?
A. Ice scream!

Zombie zone

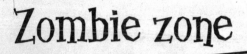

Q. What do you call a zombie who keeps pressing your doorbell?
A. A dead ringer!

Q. Why did the zombie stay home from school?
A. He was feeling rotten!

Q. What do zombies do on their holidays?
A. Take a cruise on the Dead Sea!

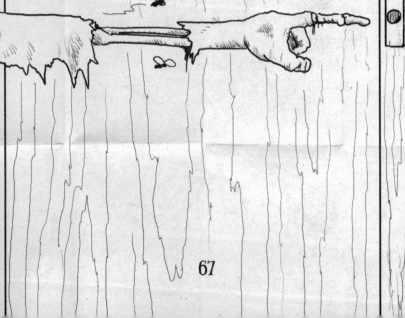

Q. What does a zombie put on his dinner?
A. Grave-y!

Q. What position do zombies normally play in a football match?
A. The ghoulie!

Q. What is the best way to stop a zombie smelling?
A. Cut off his nose!

Q. Where does the one-armed zombie like to shop?
A. At the second-hand shop!

SALE

Q. Why can't zombies bear to watch sad films?
A. Because they always cry their eyes out!

Q. What has a dog's head, a cat's tail and brains all over its face?
A. A zombie in a pet shop!

Q. What's the difference between a musician and a zombie?
A. One composes, while the other decomposes!

Q. Why was the zombie happy to be in court?
A. He was hoping the judge would give him a new life sentence!

Q. How do you know that all zombies are tired?
A. They all look dead on their feet!

Knock knock.
Who's There?
Eye Leecher.
Eye Leecher who?
Eye Leecher Brainz.

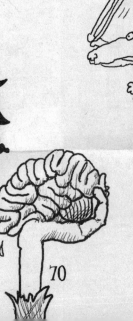

Silly skeletons

Q. Why was the skeleton so calm?
A. Nothing got under his skin!

Q. What did the skeleton want for dinner?
A. Spare ribs!

Q. Why do skeletons hate winter?
A. The cold goes right through them!

71

Q. What is a skeleton's favourite musical instrument?
A. A trombone!

Q. How do you make a skeleton laugh?
A. Tickle his funny bone!

Q. Why did the skeleton go on holiday?
A. So he could get a skele-tan!

Q. What do skeletons say before they eat?
A. Bone appétit!

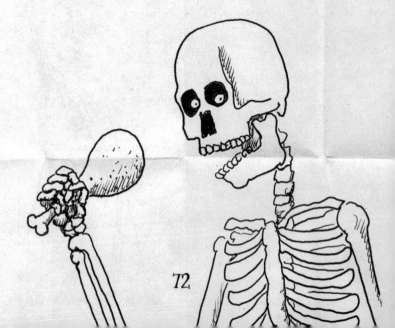

Q. What type of art do skeletons like?
A. Skull-ptures!

Q. What happened to the skeleton who got kicked in both shins?
A. He didn't have a leg to stand on!

Q. Why did the skeleton go to hospital?
A. To have his ghoul stones removed!

Q. What kind of plate does a skeleton eat off?
A. Bone china!

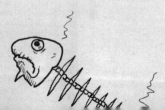

Wild witches

Q. How do you make a witch scratch?
A. Take away the 'w'!

Q. Did you hear about the witch who lost her left arm and left leg in an accident?
A. She's all right now!

Q. What do you call a witch with a frog in her hair?
A. Lily!

Q. What do witches put on their bagels?
A. Scream cheese!

Q. What type of shoe does a witch wear in summer?
A. Open-toad sandals!

Q. What happened when the little witch was naughty at school?
A. She was ex-spelled!

Q. Why won't an angry witch fly her broomstick?
A. Because she is afraid of flying off the handle!

Q. How does a witch tell the time?
A. She looks at her witch-watch!

Q. What does a speedy witch ride on?
A. A *broom-broom*stick!

Q. What do you call a witch at the seaside?
A. A sand-witch!

Knock Knock.
Who's there?
Witch.
Witch who?
Witch one of you can fix this broomstick?

Q. Who turns out the lights
at Halloween?
A. The lights witch!

Q. What do you get if you cross a witch
and ice?
A. A cold spell!

Q. What do witches put on their hair?
A. Scare-spray!

Q. What kind of horses do witches ride?
A. Night-mares!

Ghastly ghosts

Q. What do you get if you cross Bambi and a ghost?
A. Bamboo!

Q. Where do you find ghost snails?
A. At the end of ghosts' toes!

Q. Why did the ghost go for a ride in a lift?
A. He wanted to lift his spirits!

Q. Where do ghosts go
when they feel sick?
A. To the witch doctor!

Q. Why are ghosts bad liars?
A. Because you can see right
through them!

Q. What road has the most ghosts
haunting it?
A. A dead end!

Q. Where do baby ghosts go while their
parents are at work?
A. The day-scare centre!

Q. What room is useless for a ghost?
A. A living room!

Q. What do short-sighted ghosts wear?
A. Spooktacles!

Q. How do you flatten a ghost?
A. With a spirit level!

Knock Knock.
Who's there?
Emma.
Emma who?
Emma 'fraid of ghosts!

Q. What types of ghosts haunt hospitals?
A. Surgical spirits!

Q. Where do ghosts go on holiday?
A. Wails!

Q. Which ghosts made friends with the three bears?
A. Ghouldilocks!

Q. What type of tune does a ghost play on a piano?
A. A haunting melody!

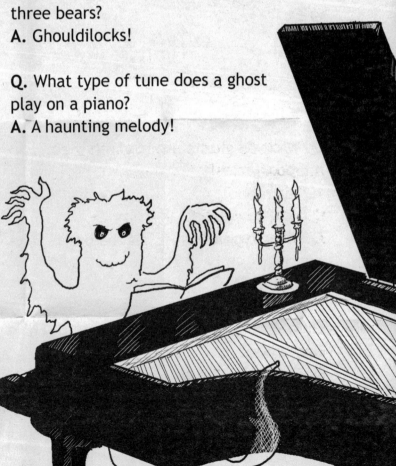

Q. What do ghosts use to clean their hair?
A. Sham-boo!

Q. What type of ghost has the best hearing?
A. The eeriest!

Q. What did the father ghost say to the baby ghost?
A. Only spook when you are spooken to!

Q. What is a ghost's favourite fruit?
A. Boo-berries!

Q. What do ghosts call their mums and dads?
A. Transparents!

Knock Knock.
Who's there?
Ice cream.
Ice cream who?
Ice cream every time I see a ghost!

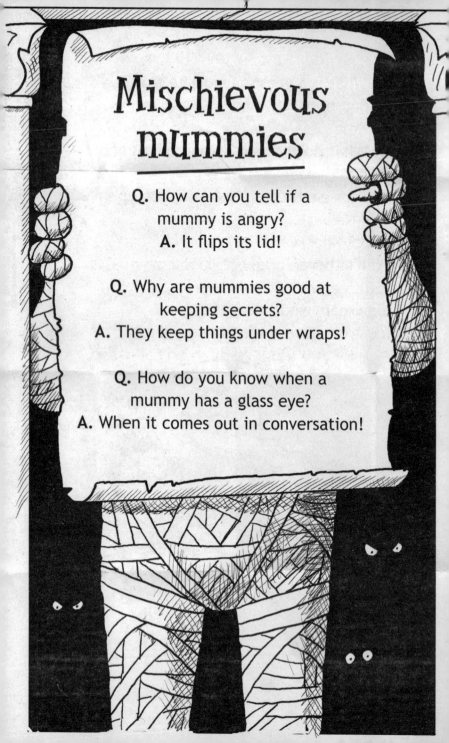

Mischievous mummies

Q. How can you tell if a
mummy is angry?
A. It flips its lid!

Q. Why are mummies good at
keeping secrets?
A. They keep things under wraps!

Q. How do you know when a
mummy has a glass eye?
A. When it comes out in conversation!

Q. Why don't mummies have many friends?
A. Because they are too wrapped up in themselves!

Q. What type of music do mummies like to listen to?
A. Wrap!

Q. Why don't mummies go on holidays?
A. They're frightened that they'll unwind!

Monster mayhem

Q. How did the monster dentist become a brain surgeon?
A. His drill slipped!

Q. Which monster can really get up your nose?
A. The Bogey Man!

Q. What type of monster eats faster than all the others?
A. A goblin!

Q. What do you call a beautiful and charming monster?
A. A failure!

Q. What is a monster's favourite bean?
A. A human bean!

Q. Why did they build a big fence around the graveyard?
A. Because people were dying to get in!

FULL

Q. How do monsters tell the future?
A. They read the horror-scopes!

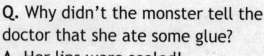

Q. What do sea monsters eat?
A. Fish and ships!

Q. Why didn't the monster tell the doctor that she ate some glue?
A. Her lips were sealed!

Q. What monster plays tricks on Halloween?
A. Prank-enstein!

Q. How do you stop a monster from biting his nails?
A. Give him some screws!

Q. Why was the monster described as temperamental?
A. He was half temper and half mental!

Q. How did the monster carpenter break his teeth?
A. He chewed his nails!

Q. What is a monster's favourite ballet?
A. Swamp lake!

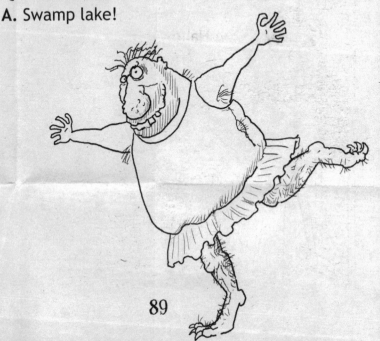

Q. What's big, scary and has three wheels?
   A. A monster riding a tricycle!

Q. Where do monsters go to send letters?
A. The ghost office!

Q. Why was the executioner late for work?
A. He was busy writing his chopping list!

Q. How did
the monster
make a Swiss roll?
A. He pushed him off
the side of a mountain!

Q. What did the monster
eat after having all his teeth
cleaned?
A. The dentist!

Q. Why did the monster push his friend
under a steamroller?
A. He wanted a flat-mate!

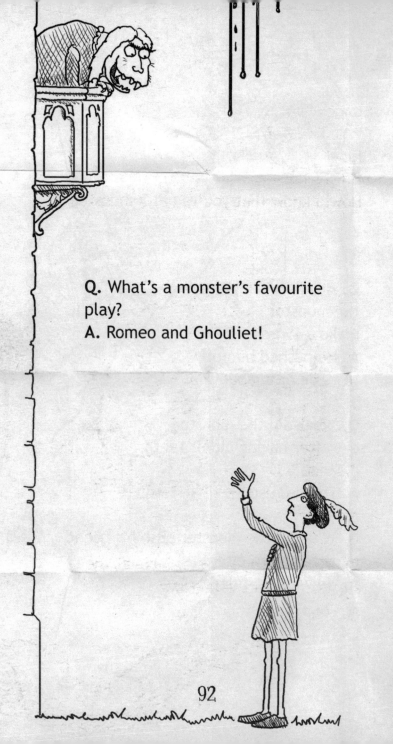

Q. What's a monster's favourite play?
A. Romeo and Ghouliet!

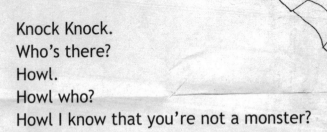

Knock Knock.
Who's there?
Howl.
Howl who?
Howl I know that you're not a monster?

Q. What did the monster have at the all-you-can-eat restaurant?
A. The waiters!

Also available

Gigglers

SCHOOL JOKES

OVER **300** JOKES

SIR, THE DOG ATE MY HOMEWORK